Table of Contents

Introduction

The recent legalization of marijuana in several states has been an unprecedented process.By legalizing both recreational and medical marijuana, states have opened up a new industry—one that people are clamoring to take advantage of. For entrepreneurs who aren't afraid to roll up their sleeves, cut through a decent chunk of bureaucratic tape, and hand over some cash up front, opening a medical dispensary is a great opportunity. A dispensary will allow you to be a pioneer in what is soon to be a massive, national industry. Marijuana Business Daily projects revenue generated by dispensaries and retail stores reached between $6.5 and $8 billion in 2019. If you are one of the many entrepreneurs interested in opening a marijuana dispensary, this book can guide you through the necessary steps.

Writing A Business Plan For A Cannabis Company

It's a very exciting time in the cannabis industry right now. Legal cannabis generated $16 billion in total economic output in the United States in 2017, and research indicates it will increase 150 percent by 2021, according to a report from cannabis industry analysts Arcview Market Research, in partnership with BDS Analytics. So how do you get a foothold in this sunrise industry? With so many people jumping on the seemingly lucrative cannabis bandwagon, it is important for you to carefully think through your cannabis company before starting. In legal states, the markets have become so saturated that cannabis companies can end up with thousands of pounds of unsold product. Write your business plan and develop your business model with this in mind so you can avoid these issues. You can choose from a few different types of business plans depending on your needs. If you're seeking investment, you need a traditional business plan. If you simply want to map out the aspects of your business for internal use, you can consider a Lean Business Plan. This guide will walk you through the steps of how to write a full business plan for your cannabis company. Remember that a business plan is a living document. You should revisit it on a regular basis as your cannabis company grows. Set time aside to sit down and revise the plan, comparing forecasts to actuals and revising as necessary. It is also a good idea to write a formal business plan to prove your professionalism. You can overcome stigma and stereotypes by demonstrating that you have a clear, viable idea for selling a product that consumers want and enjoy.

Executive Summary

Your executive summary needs to be concise. Keep it to 1 to 2 pages. But don't neglect it. Investors will read this section closely to make sure your company will be a good investment for them. It should describe your company, what you do, and what you want from the readers of your executive summary. Once finished, it could stand alone as a summary of your full-length business plan. Make sure to include information for investors who do not know much about the cannabis industry. Ganjapreneur recommends including polls about the increased demand for cannabis legalization. Your executive summary will include the following sections:

• Who you are: Your business name, location, and contact information.

• What you offer and the problem your business solves: What does your company offer and why is it needed? This is your value proposition.

• Target market: Who is your ideal buyer? Be specific.

• Competition: Who else offers similar services?

• Team: Who is on your management team?

• Financial Summary: Explain your business model, startup costs, revenues, and liabilities to the company. Mention your funding needs.

• Milestones and traction: How have you validated that there's a need for your company in your location?

Position your company's opportunity

The next few sections contain the broad overview of the opportunity your cannabis company will take advantage of. As mentioned, the industry is exploding right now. With the rise of new cannabis companies, it is important to differentiate your cannabis company from the competition, whether you are opening a farm, extraction operation, or dispensary. You can no longer rely on hype to open a successful cannabis company. You need to sell a unique/quality product or service. Set yourself apart by offering products and services that meet an unfilled need in the market. Products have become more and more diverse, and you can offer a range of flower, pre-rolls, vaporizers, concentrates, edibles, topicals, tinctures, accessories, and more. Think outside the box when it comes to seizing your opportunity and making your cannabis brand distinct. Suggestions include opening a unique edibles line, or getting a foothold in the new "bud and breakfast" cannabis-friendly lodging industry. There are also products closely related to cannabis that you can explore, such as CBD oils and hemp. The global market for CBD oils is expanding due to their medical efficacy. Also, think about the specific business model for your company. Common small business types in the cannabis industry include:

• Cannabis producers: The farmers or growing operations who grow the plants and sell them to companies

• Cannabis processors: The middlemen who take the plants from the producers and prepare them to become recreational or medical products, such as extraction operations

• Cannabis retailers: The businesses that sell the products to consumers, such as dispensaries

There are also a wide array of ancillary businesses you can enter. These include delivery, advertising, paraphernalia, and more. These businesses can sometimes be more lucrative—they do not deal directly with cannabis so they are subject to fewer regulations. A number of cannabis tech companies have also begun to take advantage of the opportunity in the marketplace.

Problem and solution

Describe the problem you have identified and how your cannabis company, whether you are a grower, processor, or retailer, solves that problem.

The problem: For example, imagine a city with an abundance of dispensaries, often upwards of three within a few blocks of each other. The problem is that they sell extremely similar products, and customers in the area are becoming more adventurous and seeking variety.

The solution: You decide to open a boutique dispensary that sells a variety of high-end edibles as well as topicals. Your products are high-quality on their own, and infused with high-quality cannabis. You provide extensive customer service and a variety of rewards options for customers. As a result, your pricing is higher than surrounding dispensaries, but you seek to brand yourself in such a way that your target market will expect higher prices for your quality of product.

TAM, SAM, and SOM: This refers to your total available market (TAM), segmented available market (SAM), and share of the market (SOM). Here, you are looking at the difference between targeting everyone (all the people who are 21 or older in your area), versus your ideal clients (people who are willing to pay your prices for your specific cannabis products), versus the number of customers you think you can realistically reach within your first few years of business. Legality will impact your TAM. You might have a greater TAM for more widely legal products, such as hemp and CBD oils. The idea here is that not everyone will be an ideal customer. Some sources recommend using social media and demographic information to learn who your ideal customer is. Once you identify your ideal customer, you can tailor your marketing and sales plan to that person.

Buyer persona: Create a character who represents your ideal client. If you are a grower, you are looking to sell to a business, not an individual. What is the ideal kind of business for you to sell to?

Key customers: If you are mainly selling to consumers, you can skip this section and move on. It is more important for companies who are selling to other businesses, like a grower. Provide details about the dispensaries or other cannabis companies that buy your product. Talk about how they are critical to your success.

Competition and competition matrix: List competitors and analyze what makes them competitive. Once again, the cannabis industry is oversaturated right now. What differentiates your cannabis company from the one down the street? Will you offer a broader array of products? Or maybe you will offer great in-store customer service, with lots of advising for which products fit customers' lifestyles.

Future products and services: Name the products/services you will offer as your company earns more money and as your market develops new needs. For instance, you might provide a delivery service and send products to customers' doorsteps. Maybe your company will develop an app to complement its website, with opportunities for customers to make social connections with each other, such as seeking smoking buddies, etc.

Execution: How Your Company Will Respond To Opportunity

The execution section describes how you will maximize the opportunity for your business. Components of this section include:

• Your marketing and sales plan

• Strategic partnerships or alliances

• Your operations plan

• Your team and company information

• Financial plan

• Milestones and metrics that you'll need to hit to be viable

• Your key assumptions and risks

• Your funding ask and exit strategy, if applicable

Marketing and sales plan

This section describes how you will attract more of your ideal customers. Include these details in your marketing and sales plan:

• Positioning: Describe how you will present your company to the market with your positioning statement. Use this model to help: "For [target market description] who [target market need], [how our business offering meets the need]. Unlike [key competition], it [most distinguishing feature].

• Pricing: Picking pricing for a dispensary can be a tricky process. You want to consider your target market and your competition when doing so. If your prices are higher than the competition's, you want to make sure you are adding value by providing something they don't or catering to a different target market. You may consider higher pricing if you sell more specialty products in a more affluent area. Finally, pricing can be difficult given the number of products being sold that are new to the market, with little data yet collected as to their performance. Try generating interest in new products with special deals such as discounts on complementary products. BDS Analytics has also generated some area-specific reports on cannabis pricing.

• Promotion: Explain your advertising plan and marketing tactics, whether they are online, print, or networking.

• Strategic alliances: List any people or organizations with whom you are working, such as third-party listing sites. Valuable strategic alliances for a cannabis company might include security staff, pharmacists, attorneys, sales associates, and store managers.

In addition to other digital marketing tactics, your cannabis company should have its own website. It is important to showcase your products with visuals. Consider adding a "menu" with a list of products divided into categories. Include pictures of each product. It's also a nice touch to customize the site with search boxes for recreational products and medical products, respectively, as well as for indicas, sativas, and hybrids. And remember: don't market your cannabis to or near minors. Solely market it to those who are 21 and over. Often, customers cannot distinguish one brand of cannabis from another, so your most important marketing tactic is to build relationships with your customers and provide them with excellent service.

Operations

• Sourcing and fulfillment: If you are a dispensary, who grows your cannabis and acts as your vendor? If you grow cannabis, who do you sell it to? Extraction operations?

Dispensaries? A dispensary will need both a storefront where customers view and purchase products, as well as a storage space for products that are not on the shelf yet. You must make sure your dispensary is on a compliant property. Different areas have different laws about compliant properties, such as a minimum legal distance from schools, churches, and residential areas. Consult an attorney to make sure your storefront occupies a compliant property.

• Technology: Consider your plans for labeling and packaging your product, and establish an inventory system. For growers, consider growing cycles, climate, and the different production profiles of indoor, outdoor, and greenhouse operations. If you are in the extraction end of the business, read up on technologies that will optimize your operations.

• Distribution: Transportation within the cannabis industry remains a developing phenomenon, like many aspects of the industry. Some companies, such as TransCanna, are pioneering transportation and distribution methods from cannabis manufacturers to consumers. For a product that goes bad before you sell it, the legal methods of disposal are burning or composting.

Set start dates, end dates, and budgets for specific milestones, for before and after you launch your business. Set measurable, achievable milestones. Milestones can be about any aspect of your cannabis company as long as they emphasize growth. For metrics, decide which numbers to check regularly to track your company's health. Metrics for a cannabis company might include:

• Repeat customers

• The rate at which products are selling

• Vendors' pricing (for a dispensary purchasing from a vendor)

• Dispensaries' ability to buy your product at its pricing (for a grower selling to a dispensary)

This section should also include details about past successes (traction) and risks:

• Traction: Look back at major milestones you have achieved. Hopefully, they demonstrate that your business model works and that you are filling a need for your market. If you're looking to attract private funders, this section is important since it shows your initial success.

• Key assumptions and risks: Acknowledge the assumptions you are basing your business on. Set out to prove them right if you can. Also, discuss risks so that investors know you have considered what could go wrong and that you have a plan for dealing with challenges. As mentioned, thickets of legal complications surround the cannabis industry. Demonstrate that you have familiarized yourself with local policies and sought legal counsel. Furthermore, a glut of cannabis companies have arrived on the scene recently. Back up with market research why you stand out from your competitors and are here to stay.

Team

Management team and qualifications: Address who works for you, what do they do, and how much you pay them. Compile the details of their relevant experience and education.

Hiring plans: Outline what positions you might need to hire to fill skills gaps in your management team and how much you plan to pay them.

Company overview

In this section, include the following information about your company's legal and organizational structure.

• Mission statement: Your mission statement articulates your goals for what your company does for its customers, employees, and owners. It will read something like this: "Our mission is to provide X (services) for Y (customers) by Z (methods)."

• Intellectual property: List any patents you have or have pending, and mention any core technology you are licensing from another company. Be sure to avoid copyright infringement when you create images and advertisements for marketing your company.

• A review of your company's legal structure and ownership: Explain your business structure and who owns how much of it. Pay attention to the legalities around cannabis in your state. The National Organization for the Reform of Marijuana Laws, or NORML, also compiled a database of laws and regulations around cannabis in each state. Additionally, check out these tables from the National Conference of State Legislatures.

• The business location: Describe the company's location and any facilities it owns. If you work as a grower as well as a retailer, include both your farm/greenhouse and your store location. Successful dispensaries tend to go on to open more than one location.

A brief history of the startup if it's an existing company: This provides background for potential new employees.

Financial plan

Your financial plan helps you track your finances so you can accurately gauge your business's performance. Include these key elements:

• Profit and loss statement: This explains how your business made a profit or incurred a loss in a given amount of time (typically three months) by listing all revenue and expenses, then documenting the total amount of net profit or loss.

• Cash flow statement: Documentation of how much cash the business brought in, how much it paid out, and the amount of its ending cash balance (on a monthly basis).

• Balance sheet: Snapshots how your company is performing at a given moment by including how much money you have in the bank, how much your customers owe you, and how much you owe your vendors.

• Sales forecast: Projections of what you think you will sell in a given timeframe (1 to 3 years).

• Business ratios: Comparisons of your company's financials with numbers from the industry profile.

• Personnel plan: Costs of employees.

• Use of funds: Needed if you're seeking investment or a loan. This section explains how you will use investors' money, whether for marketing or purchasing inventory.

• Exit strategy: Needed if you're seeking investment. This section includes a brief plan for how you will eventually sell your company. You could sell it to another company or to the public. List a few companies you might eventually sell to. This is important to investors because it tells them how they will make money from their investment when you leave.

Opening a cannabis company can incur additional expenses, such as the cost of hiring an attorney who can help you navigate complex laws and regulations.

Familiarize yourself with license and permit information as much as possible, but also seek professional legal counsel. Banks typically will not fund a cannabis startup. Due to federal regulations, they must report every transaction involving funds derived from illegal activity—and despite state legalizations, cannabis is still considered federally illegal. Instead, seek private investors to give your cannabis company the money it needs for startup costs. There are a multitude of websites designed to help connect cannabis entrepreneurs with investors. Also, consider personal and private loans. If you are a grower, see if certain grants or other means of funding work for you. You also typically cannot use banks to deposit the profits from your cannabis company. Some smaller credit unions have begun to open checking accounts expressly for the cannabis industry. MoneyTrac provides dispensaries with kiosks where customers can make cashless payments. However, prepare to come up with strategies for tracking and storing large amounts of cash for your cannabis business, because these banks remain rare. Consider investing in a safe and security measures such as cameras, if you go that route. For more, check out this article on how to accept payments as a cannabis business to help you assess your options.

Opening A Marijuana Dispensary

Understanding the legal risks

Despite the increasing number of states that have legalized medical (and recreational) marijuana use, there are risks. Marijuana is still considered illegal at the federal level. Medical cannabis is classified as a Schedule 1 drug under the federal Controlled Substance Act. This means that it's classified as a potential drug use product, and it can only be suggested, not prescribed. There's not much case law on this topic so the true legal status of dispensaries (when it comes to federal law) is cloudy. This can make it difficult for a dispensary to know how to stay within legal parameters, which in turn can expose your business to legal risks. (This is one reason we suggest including a lawyer well-versed in this type of venture when building your team.)

Financial risks

It's not news that opening a business takes a substantial financial investment. When considering cannabis retail, there are some additional challenges to obtaining the financial backing needed. Securing funding in the cannabis industry has proven to be very difficult through traditional methods, and due to risks, most banks won't even allow you to transaction your cannabis business through them. This can mean having to operate your business on a cash basis, which can make you more susceptible to theft. It will take some creativity on your part, and perhaps the entire contents of your savings, to get the ball rolling. The capital required to open a dispensary can be upwards of $250,000 – $750,000.

Eligibility

Are you qualified? Local governments have a series of "must-haves" in order to apply to be a dispensary owner, as well as red flags that will disqualify you immediately. NORML has a good resource to look up marijuana laws and license requirements by state to get a full understanding of whether you are eligible and what you'll need. In general, a few standard requirements include:

• Owner, investors and license holders may not have any felony convictions

• Dispensary location must be more than 500-1000 feet away from schools, churches, and other restricted locations (varies by state)

• Must have a complete business plan with an outline of property ownership, costs, business licenses, etc.

• Compliance with all safety regulations

Research Policies, Legalities, Licensing, Cost, And Location

So, you are pretty convinced this is for you, but you have more questions. This is the time to jump into research and answer those burning questions.

• What are the laws in my state for dispensing and use?

• Would my business be protected by state laws?

• What are the costs associated with starting a dispensary?

• What licenses and applications are required?

State laws for cannabis use and dispensing vary. According to the NCSL (National Conference of State legislators) as of June 24, 2019: A total of 34 states, District of Columbia, Guam, Puerto Rico and US Virgin Islands have approved a comprehensive, publicly available medical marijuana/cannabis programs. Approved efforts in 12 states allow use of "low THC, high cannabidiol (CBD)" products for medical reasons in limited situations or as a legal defense. See Table 2 below for more information about those programs. Low-THC programs are not counted as comprehensive medical marijuana programs. NCSL uses criteria similar to other organizations tracking this issue to determine if a program is "comprehensive":

• Protection from criminal penalties for using marijuana for a medical purpose;

• Access to marijuana through home cultivation, dispensaries or some other system that is likely to be implemented;

• It allows a variety of strains or products, including those with more than "low THC;" and

• It allows either smoking or vaporization of some kind of marijuana products, plant material or extract, and

• Is not a limited trial program. (South Dakota and Nebraska have limited, trial programs that are not open to the public.)

Licenses

Paperwork. It's probably the least exciting part of starting a new business — but often times the most important. When starting a dispensary, you want that paper trail of protection. So, what exactly is required? That depends where you live. Let's take a look at California's requirements:

• Seller's Permit: Like other businesses selling goods, individuals and startups interested in selling cannabis or cannabis products will need to register for a seller's permit. This is a basic prerequisite when applying for a cannabis dispensary license.

• Cannabis duration license: There are two types. Temporary (up to 120 days) and non-temporary (which must be renewed every 12 months)

• Cannabis dispensary license: Nonrefundable dispensary application fees generally range from $1,000 to $5,000, with registration or annual fees typically between $5,000 and $20,000.

In order to be approved for a dispensary license in Florida, you must have the following plans in order:

• Business Plan

• Cultivation Plan

• Marijuana Processing and Manufacturing Plan

• Employee Manual

• Environmental Plan

• Financial Plan

• Fire Safety Plan

• Inventory Control Plan

• Recordkeeping Plan

• Patient Education Plan

• Product Safety Plan

- Security Plan

- Staffing Plan

- Suitability of Proposed Plan

- Transportation Plan

The license rates and tax fees vary state by state. Drastically. For example, in Louisiana, the licensing fee is $150, while New Jersey applicants must fork out a staggering $20,000.

Insurance

Insurance is the best way to protect your hard work against fire, damage, and theft. You'll want to protect your investment with the proper insurance:

- General liability: typically required by landlords and at a state level. This protects against general damages and injuries.

- Product liability: this covers inventory and dispensary equipment.

- Medicine: Medicinal coverage protects inventory against fire or theft both in your brick and mortar location, as well as during transportation from manufacturer to your storefront.

As this fantastic industry grows, so do the insurance companies willing to protect your business assets.

Medicinal but not a prescription. Because medical cannabis can only be suggested and not prescribed, it is not protected by FDA tax exemptions. This means that the product will be required to be issued a state tax.

Cannabis Training

You now have a strong understanding of the risks and requirements to start a dispensary. You are eager and willing to jump in and get your hands dirty. Before you begin to sign those application checks over — make sure you understand your product. Educating yourself on various forms of cannabis, your customer base and how your product will benefit them is essential. Hemp Staff shares, when customers come in, they may be anxious or nervous about trying medical marijuana. This is especially true if they have never used cannabis before. Your job is to both reassure and show them which products work the best for their problem. Working at a dispensary means your clients need to learn to trust you and your knowledge. They gain that trust by purchasing products that you recommend that work. Therefore, you need to come to interviews prepared to give excellent advice and demonstrate your knowledge of the plant. Consider taking a dispensary training course, to grasp a firm understanding of the products you will be selling. Doing so will educate yourself and your employees on cannabinoids and which specifically to recommend based on clients' needs. Founded in 2007, Oaksterdam University was the first cannabis college, with educational roots going back to 1995. OU boasts over 40,000 Alumni worldwide. The primary focus on their programs is a full-spectrum look at the cannabis industry from business to botany. Oaksterdam prides itself on being a leader in training in the canna industry, emphasizing that this new emerging world of cannabis dispensaries can be both transformational as well as transactional.

Write A Business Plan

Studies show that entrepreneurs who take the time to write a business plan are 2.5 times more likely to follow through and get their business off the ground. Traditional business plans have the following sections:

• An executive summary. This section summaries the entire plan, so it is generally written last. Anyone reading your plan will read this first, so it's an important element.

• An industry overview. This section gives a brief overview of the industry sector your business will operate in. It includes key players, industry trends, and estimates of industry sales.

• Market analysis. This looks at the target market for your product or service. It has a breakdown of your market segments, their geographic location, and what their needs are. This section shows anyone reading that you have a thorough understanding of the people you plan to sell to or serve.

• Competitive analysis. Who are your direct and indirect competitors? How do they currently meet your target market's needs, and how will you differentiate your product or services?

• Sales and marketing plan. What is your unique selling proposition? How are you going to promote your business and persuade your target audience to buy? This section goes into detail on questions like these.

• Management plan. This section outlines your legal and management structure. It shows who your leadership team is and what your staffing needs will be. If you plan to seek funding, you should describe your advisory board here, as well.

• Operating plan. Your business location, facilities, equipment, and what kind of employees you'll need are in this section. Any suppliers, manufacturing processes, and any other operating details also appear here.

• Financial plan. This section is for all things financial. There are three key financial documents of any business that go here: an income statement, a balance sheet, and a cash flow statement.

• Appendices and Exhibits. Any information that helps support your business idea goes here, including market studies, legal agreements, photos of your products, and more.

A good business plan guides you through each stage of starting and managing your business.

Acquire Funding

Financing any business can be a headache. Funding a medical dispensary can be a full-bodied migraine. Because, marijuana is still not legal at the federal level, it's more difficult for owners of medical marijuana dispensaries to apply for loans, merchant accounts, or receive other types of financing to cover operating expenses. The cost of opening a dispensary really vary depending on the county, city, and state requirements. Startup investment averages between $250,000 to $750,000. This sum can include everything from securing insurance, hiring employees, and renting a storefront. If you've been fortunate enough to find an investor to hand over this kind of cash, congratulations! If not, don't fret — there are other options!

Is traditional banking an option?

In short, probably not. Because of the federal illegality of cannabis, most financial institutions will not consider investing in an effort to protect themselves. A dispensary is considered a high-risk venture, and even if you were able to find a financial institution ready to back you, the increased costs and fees can quickly make doing business with them unprofitable. Merchant Maverick explains:

• Banks are insured by the Federal Deposit Insurance Corporation. A bank that works with companies that violate federal law will not be insured by the FDIC. This includes medical marijuana dispensaries. Instead of taking on this risk, most banks opt to simply avoid working with businesses in the cannabis industry.

• There are also legal issues that a bank could potentially face when working with businesses in the cannabis industry. For example, a bank could be charged with money laundering for accepting deposits from a medical marijuana dispensary. Although the odds of this law being enforced are slim, lenders simply don't want to take that risk.

Alternate Funding Options

If you find yourself being turned down by banks and other financial facilities, you are going to need some alternative ways to start your business. Sure, funding can be more challenging to acquire, but, as hundreds of small business owners can attest, it is possible! You just may need to get a little creative!

Equity Funding

Equity funding is gaining popularity as the canna-market continues to increase. Equity financing is the process of raising capital through the sale of shares. Companies raise money by selling shares of ownership in their company in return for cash. Equity financing for your new business can come from many sources; for example, personal friends and family, and investors. Fundera shares three main types of equity funding: Venture Capital, Angel Investors, and crowdfunding.

• Venture Capital: There are a handful of venture capital firms that focus specifically on cannabis startups, including Snoop Dogg's Casa Verde Capital. If you're beyond the seed funding stage, then these firms can be worth a try. New Cannabis Ventures has a list of VCs, and a quick Google search can also turn up some results, too.

• Angel Investors: Just like there are plenty of VC firms looking to invest, cannabis has peaked the interest of angel investors, too. To find your angel, you can start by checking out AngelList, which actually has a section dedicated to helping startups find angels who are interested in investing in marijuana. An offline option is to try tapping your network or any angels you may have previously worked with to see if they can point you in the right direction. Cannabis industry conventionsand meetups also exist, and it never hurts to attend some and see who you connect with.

• Crowdfunding: Crowdfunding has recently arisen as a popular option for funding startups. The two most well-known platforms are Indiegogo and Kickstarter. Indiegogo, for one, has approved some cannabis companies to raise funds on their platform. StartEngine, a lesser-known platform, has also approved weed startups. Finally, there are a couple marijuana-specific platforms, including CannaFundr and Fundanna.

Debt Funding

Startup costs funded by debt, be it loans or business credit can be tricky to secure – but new alternative lenders have been able to assist entrepreneurs in getting the funding they needed.

Personal Loans

If you have a good credit score and steady income, you may qualify for a personal loan to help with start-up costs. Personal loans are the option many startups choose because the industry, time in business, and usage of funds aren't taken into consideration for loan approval. You will, however, have to disclose how the funds will be used.

Credit Cards

A business credit card is a good (but very expensive if you don't pay it off monthly) option. They can be utilized to pay recurring expenses, cover an emergency, or pay for startup costs.

Build A Team

Running a successful dispensary relies on much more than modern decor and a great product selection. As Henry Ford said, "If everyone is moving forward together, then success takes care of itself." When it comes to building the best team possible at your shop, you need to think about two types of individuals – your professional support that works behind the scenes and your day-to-day staff. If both groups are both trustworthy and skilled, you will find yourself on the fast track toward success!

Professional Support

The truth is your dispensary will have a lot of moving pieces that require support your clients will know nothing about. As the business owner, your most critical interest is to be sure everything is being done correctly with your I's dotted and t's crossed. As with most businesses, two of the most vital people to add to your team are a lawyer and a CPA. Blogger Dave Emmett writes,

• Knowing how to open a dispensary can be challenging; it often requires that you deal with a lot of red tape, and it helps to have someone who can make sure you're doing things by the book.

• Speaking of books, given that dispensaries must adhere to specific tax codes, it's best to hire a trained professional to keep an eye on the numbers.

• Many dispensaries hire a compliance officer, as these individuals make it their business to follow all regulations to the letter.

The front end of the dispensary, the end that helps clients is equally as important. You should employ the following to help with day-to-day operations.

• Budtenders: Budtenders have to be qualified to work in a dispensary and must have a wide range of cannabis knowledge. In order to provide customers with a positive experience at a dispensary, budtenders need to demonstrate their knowledge of strains, cannabis products, and medical use.

• Managers: Aim to find someone who has experience in the cannabis industry. They should have a passion for the industry and be someone who can manage your team when you are not around.

• Administrative Assistant: bookkeeping, accounts payable and receivable, or in-house IT.

• Security: Security detail is required by some states, but a good idea for all. Security will protect your employees, customers, and investments.

• Board of Directors/Influencers: When adding to trusted business associates to put on a board of directors, consider adding a physician to oversee the entire patient care process.

Secure A Location

When it's time to find the perfect location — understand that when it comes to dispensary real estate, "perfect" will be synonymous with "compliant". As with most things' cannabis-related, compliance codes vary from state to state.

Renting vs. Buying

Renting, for now, is a popular choice among cannabis entrepreneurs. Why? Because of the ever-changing environment of the marijuana industry, a property that is compliant now might not be in two years. A compliant property means different things in different places, and even when you find a property within regulation, you have to be upfront with the landlord about your plans to open a dispensary there, and know they might not be supportive.

Location

When searching for a place to open your dispensary, also consider if it is convenient for potential customers.

Resources to find a property

With the rise in this industry, there are real estate agencies and brokers who specialize in finding cannabis-friendly corporate spaces. Utilize some of the resources below to find a space that may work you for you:

• 420 Property is an excellent resource if you are looking to purchase a marijuana-friendly property.

• Weed Rentals specializes in corporate and private spaces for rent.

• Cannabis Real Estate Consultants specializing in corporate real estate for sale

Branding And Marketing Your Cannabis Dispensary
Brand identity

The cannabis industry is in a transition period, from what was considered a "black market" to now a legitimate medical need. Part of that transition is getting the branding right, in a way that presents medical dispensaries in an accepted and celebrated space. If your dispensary business is going to get noticed, you need to consciously develop your brand identity. As we've previously discussed, your brand is your company's public identity. Ideally, your brand should embody the best (and most essential) attributes of your company. Here are a few questions to guide you as you think about your brand:

• What personality do I want my brand to project?

• Who will want to buy my cannabis products?

• What can customers get from my cannabis products that they can't get anywhere else?

• What makes my brand unique?

• What is the most important part of my customer's experience?

Your answers to these questions (and others like them) will build the core of your brand. All of your future branding decisions should expand on these ideas. Your business name, your business logo, your website design, how you design the exterior and interior of your dispensary, and everything else visual about your brand, should all grow from the concepts you layout here. So, take the time to think – really think – about your brand from the start. And maintain that brand as your dispensary business evolves and grows. This consistency of brand personality (and the quality of your products) will keep loyal customers coming back. It is evident marijuana dealers sell the same products. There is high competition in the marijuana industry even for the best marijuana dispensary in Nevada. This can be challenging for cannabis dispensary dealers to effectively market their particular brands. This is the leading challenge marijuana marketers' face while marketing a brand's product. Here are some tips to help service providers differentiate their brand from that of other Companies:

Alternative pricing

Alternative pricing can play a vital role in differentiating a brand in a congested market. Alternative pricing is one of the quickest methods of making your brand stand out from the rest. There are three ways of conducting an alternative pricing. Here they are:

• Premium pricing: This process involves charging higher prices on your marijuana products when compared to other competitors. This technique should only apply if you are dealing with extremely high-quality cannabis and if your targeted audience can pay this price. This can make it easy for customers to differentiate your brand.

• Low pricing: This is the first option brands consider when they want to differentiate their brands from others. Low pricing can help a brand garner widespread attention that competitive brands. However, this process requires a lot of consultation before anyone can adopt it.

• Unique structure: As the name suggests, this process involves a brand offering unique services from other competitors. Unique services such as offers and discounts among others, makes it easy for a person to differentiate your brand from your fellow competitors.

Forge partnership

As earlier stated, marijuana industry is quite congested as dealers are selling similar products. This can be confusing to customers when it comes to selecting products from a certain brand. In addition to this, brand owners might find their marketing strategies failing to improve their sales. Marketing strategies fail in the marijuana industry because customers are unable to differentiate a particular brand from other competitors. A marijuana dealer can differentiate his brand other competitors from by merging up with another Company.

There are very few businesses in marijuana industry that have adopted the customer-centric culture. A customer-centric culture is important as it helps brands operate based on their clients' pleasure and dislikes. Secondly, a brand can get suggestions from its loyal customers on how to be unique. Lastly, it creates some form of uniqueness. This can make a person easily identify your brand. A marijuana dealer shouldn't worry about customers being unable to differentiate their brands with that of their fellow competitors. The above guidelines can completely solve this common occurrence.

Website

Your website is one of your dispensary's most important ambassadors. As we explained previously:

• Today, it's impossible to reach most customers without a website. This is especially true for new small businesses and startups trying to compete in an increasingly noisy world. but it's also true for even established companies.

• Don't believe me? A recent study shows that 97% of consumers research their purchases online before they buy something.

• Your website is a crucial component of your marketing and branding strategy.

So, put this vital business tool to work for your business.Start by ensuring that your website design truly embodies your brand. Visitors should be able to understand who you are and what your brand is about as soon as they arrive.Your website's visual design and marketing copy should project your brand's voice and identity. Here are some suggestions:

• Use your brand's colors.

• Prominently feature your logo.

• Share your philosophy as a dispensary.

• Write copy with your target consumer in mind.

In addition to serving as a brand ambassador, your website is also a great venue for attracting a wider customer base. Finally, strong website design will lend credibility and legitimacy to your business. Make sure you're using your website to its fullest capacity.

Marketing

As the cannabis industry grows at a rapid pace, it can feel overwhelming to keep up-to-date with the constantly-changing federal and state regulations. Advertising regulations are strict, and many marketing platforms restrict or outright ban cannabis advertisements due to the substance's federal status. The popular website Leafly, put together a state-by-state guide to cannabis advertising regulations that should help cannabis businesses adhere to the guidelines set forth by both the state they're operating in as well as any states in which they want to advertise.